Piano · Vocal · Guitar

SONGS FROM
!HERO THE ROCK OPERA

ISBN 0-634-08277-9

HAL•LEONARD®
CORPORATION
7777 W. BLUEMOUND RD. P.O. BOX 13819 MILWAUKEE, WI 53213

Visit Hal Leonard Online at
www.halleonard.com

FIRE OF LOVE

Words and Music by EDDIE DeGARMO
and BOB FARRELL

Moderate Rock

HERO:
I've lived a-mong you since I was a boy, _____ stood
They say a proph-et's nev-er known by his friends. _____ You

in this tem-ple, read the an-cient sto - ries. We have
look right at me, _____ but you don't com-pre-hend. _____ But I've

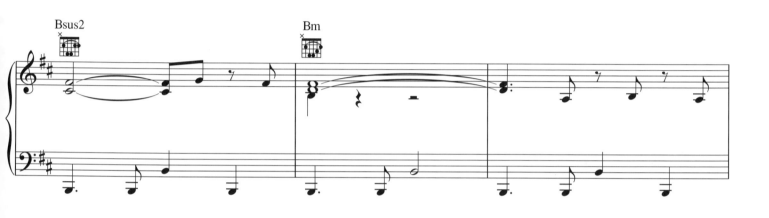

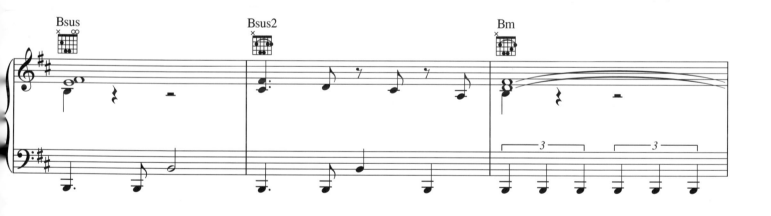

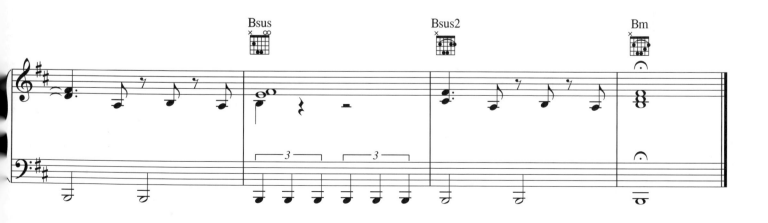

LOSE MY LIFE WITH YOU

Words and Music by EDDIE DeGARMO
and BOB FARRELL

SECRETS OF THE HEART

Words and Music by EDDIE DeGARMO
and BOB FARRELL

Has my life __ been writ - ten in the stars? __ And can you

tell me all __ I've ev - er done, __ all I've ev - er done? __ So I

all I've ev - er done? __

Se - crets of __ my heart. __

STAND UP AND WALK

Words and Music by EDDIE DeGARMO
and BOB FARRELL

CRIPPLE:

I need some change; an -
I need a hand; an -

To Coda

a - bove the game you knew. Ev - 'ry - bod - y jump; I've come___ to take your sins a - way.

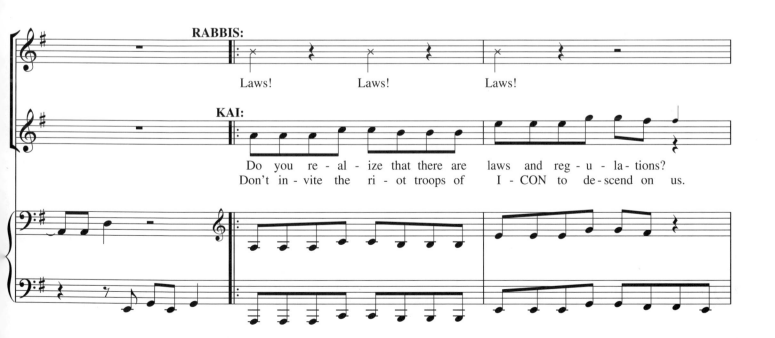

RABBIS:

Laws!   Laws!   Laws!

KAI:

Do you re - al - ize that there are   laws and reg - u - la - tions?
Don't in - vite the ri - ot troops of   I - CON to de - scend on us.

Laws! Laws! Laws! Laws! Laws!

Do you have a per-mit for these heal-ings on the Sab-bath? Let me make this or-der clear:
Don't in-cite the ur-chins to be-lieve in all those tricks you do. For all of them it's much too late; their

Laws! Laws!

Don't want your cir-cus here!

I don't want your cir-cus here.
sins al-read-y seal their fate.

Em

Em7

Harmonica solo ad lib.

LOVE'S DECLARATION

Words and Music by EDDIE DeGARMO
and BOB FARRELL

Moderately slow, in 2

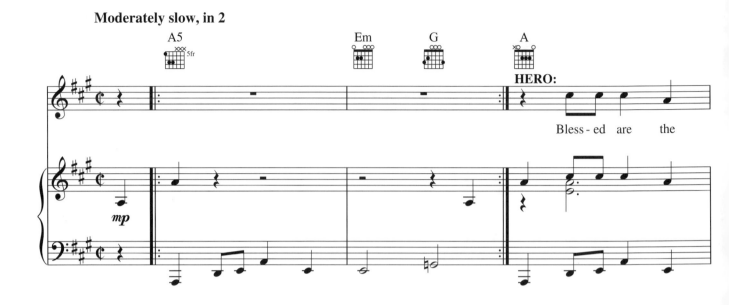

HERO:
Bless-ed are the

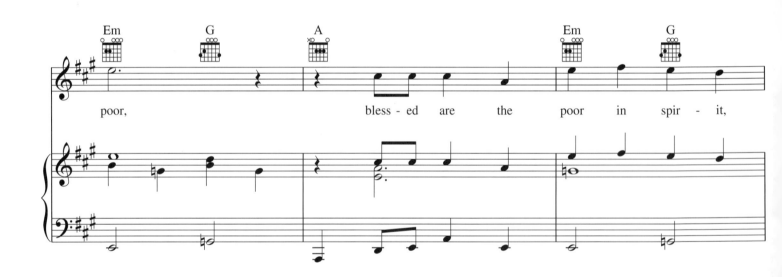

poor, bless-ed are the poor in spir-it,

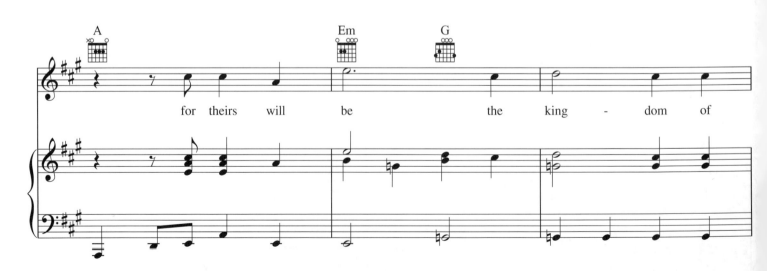

for theirs will be the king-dom of

HERO, PETROV & MAGGIE:

RAISED IN HARLEM

Words and Music by EDDIE DeGARMO,
BOB FARRELL, T-BONE and PETE STEWART

* Recorded a half step higher.

a lit - tle teen-aged girl __ who was raised in Har - lem,

JARIUS: *(Spoken) Nah, it can't be, man.*

Har -

C5

B♭sus2

JARIUS:

Play 3 times

- lem.

It just can't be, y'all.

Rap 4: *(See Rap lyrics)*

Last time: (I was

C5

B♭sus2

raised,

raised in Har - lem.) __

N.C.

Rap 3: *(See Rap lyrics)*

HERO:
I need You, God.

I know your heart is break-ing, but this girl is on-ly sleep-ing.

If you'll just give us both a min-ute or two.___ Oh yeah,___

Har - lem. ___ Raised in the cit - y of Har - lem, y'all.) ___

Rap Lyrics

Rap 1:
My people telling me that you the man
That can heal the sick wit ya healin' hand,
Demand sickness to scram
And got power like Superman,

Command the winds to cease,
Even teach priests and walk on water. If this is true,
Then I got the faith that you can heal my daughter.

I'm down on my knees beggin' ya, please,
I need a blessing. I'm tired of stressing.
Besides, my daughter's just an adolescent.

Rap 2:
My baby's dying in the streets, bleeding,
Barely breathin', about to die, Hero,
Caught up, shot up over these drugs
By some thugs, Hero.

I know I'm just a chronic breathin' heathen
That's thievin', grievin' and fendin' for
  my daughter's healin'.
But I'm still believin'
That you can find it in your heart
To help a man like me. Heal my baby
And take away her pain and this misery.

Rap 3:
I'm pleadin', Hero, just say a prayer, she'll be O.K.
I know that if you come and just
say the word to my daughter,
You'll take all the suffering away.
Just come and touch her and hug her;
I know that she'll recover.
Me and her mother love her like crazy,
'Cause we got no other.

Rap 4:
Ain't nobody dyin', Mammie, so stop the cryin'
'Cause she fi'n to live.
This is Hero, the man who came to heal our baby kid.
Just have faith and believe that He can fulfill all our needs.
Heed him indeed; he's the one who can heal our dyin' seed.
I got the faith and trust that he can save
Our baby darlin'.
From Cali to Harlem
His healin' stats are flawless and startlin'.

MANNA FROM HEAVEN

Words and Music by EDDIE DeGARMO
and BOB FARRELL

JUDE: Mag - gie, ___ these peo - ple ___ have no - where _ to go. **MAGGIE:** These

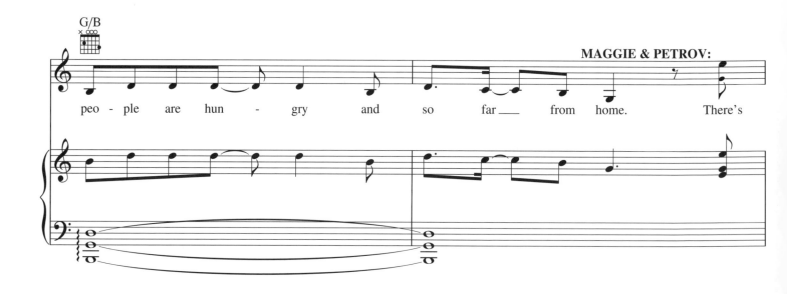

peo - ple are hun - gry and so far ___ from home. **MAGGIE & PETROV:** There's

noth - ing ___ to give them, ___ there's noth - ing ___ to eat. ___

Hey - o, hey - o, hey - o, hey - o.

Hey - o, hey - o, hey - o, hey - o. ___

Whoa, ___ whoa. ___

Hey - o, hey - o, hey - o, hey - o. Hey - o, hey - o,

D.S. al Coda

CODA

fy ex - pla - na - tion, ___ so I'll just ___ give thanks to our won - der - ful Fa - ther. ___

HERO

Words and Music by EDDIE DeGARMO
and BOB FARRELL

PETROV:

From the street I heard _ a reb-el's voice, it got _ to me. _
Don't You know it's a dan-g'rous mis-sion? Some can hurt You for the words You say. _

I could feel a strong _ wind blow-in'; change was
Love's a bea-con, but it ain't no wea-pon when trou-ble's

*Recorded a half step higher.

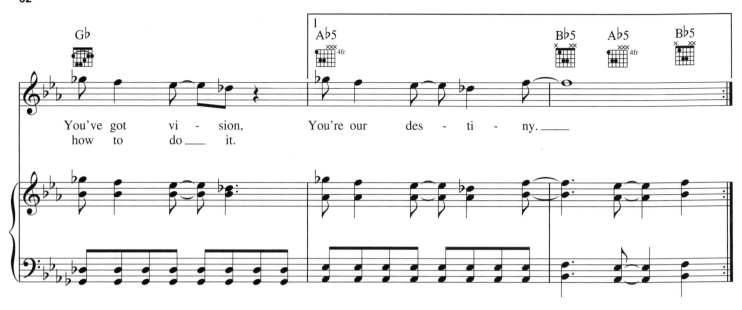

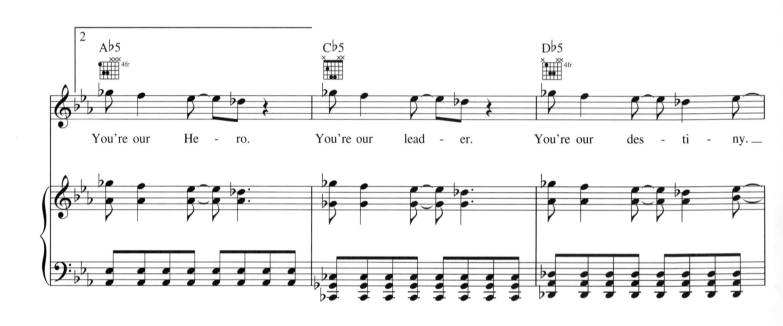

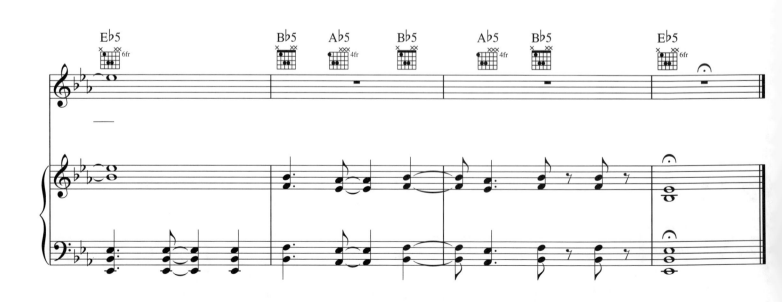

FINALLY HOME

Words and Music by EDDIE DeGARMO
and BOB FARRELL

Moderately

He has come, our lead-er who will save us all, fi-n'lly

come, a stran-ger who has heard us call. He has come, this reb-el who will

lead the fight, fi-n'lly home. He is home.

Recorded a half step lower.

NOT IN OUR HOUSE

Words and Music by EDDIE DeGARMO,
BOB FARRELL and PETE STEWART

PARTY IN THE HOUSE TODAY

Words and Music by EDDIE DeGARMO
and BOB FARRELL

Moderately

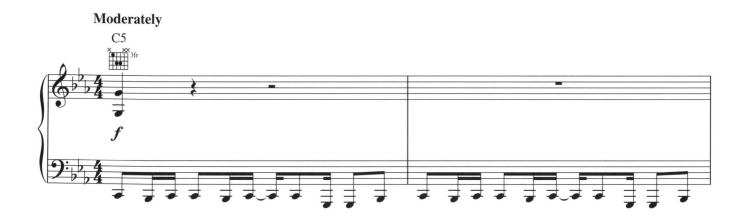

PETROV:

Well, you

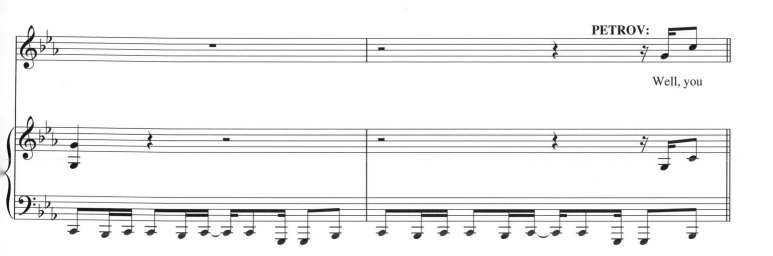

may not think__ I'm the bright-est jewel__ in this strange fra - ter - ni - ty.__ A
know we've all__ had some heav-y times.__ It's cra - zy all a - round. A pa-

Guitar solo ad lib.

Play 3 times

Let's   get this par - ty start - ed. {(1., 2.) Let's}
                                          {(3.) All}

right,   let's par-ty.   Let's get this par - ty start - ed,   right here,   right now,   in this

house,   let's par - ty.

SHADOWMAN

Words and Music by EDDIE DeGARMO
and BOB FARRELL

I AM

Words and Music by EDDIE DeGARMO
and BOB FARRELL

Moderate Rock Ballad

HERO: Some-times __ it's hard

to do what you're meant to do. __

The fi - re we must walk through, __

KILL THE HERO

Words and Music by EDDIE DeGARMO
and BOB FARRELL

Moderately slow, ominously

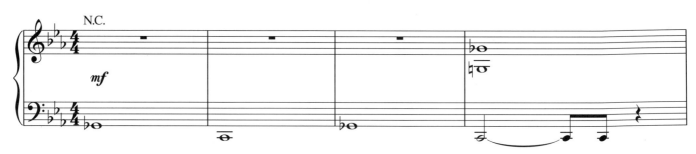

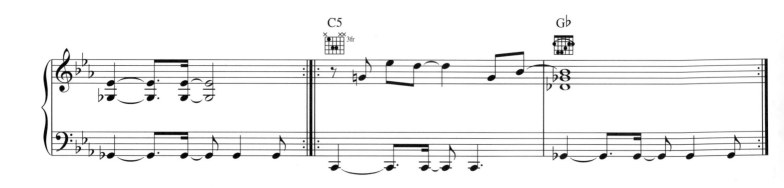

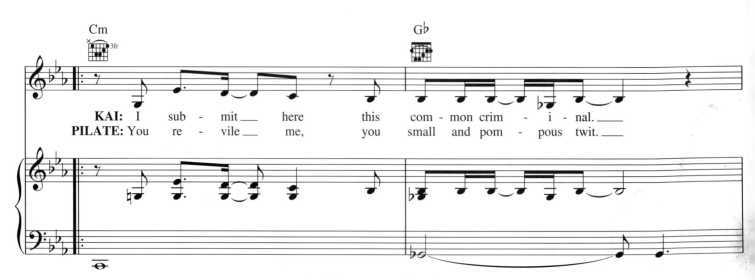

KAI: I sub - mit ___ here this com - mon crim - i - nal. ___
PILATE: You re - vile ___ me, you small and pom - pous twit. ___

PILATE: *(Spoken) Kai, I have no energy for this.*   *Devlin, take this Jew*

Hero back to Brooklyn.   *(Whispered) And maybe he doesn't make it all the way there.*

Let your street people decide his fate.

The court of ICON is hereby adjourned.

(This man is an im - pos - ter.

Ex - e - cute, ex - e - cute, ex - e - cute the He - ro.

This man is an im - pos - ter. Take a - way the He - ro. This man is an im - pos - ter.

Ex - e - cute the He - ro. The He - ro must die.) **PILATE:** *I wash my hands of this sick madness.*

HE'S NOT HERE

Words and Music by EDDIE DeGARMO
and BOB FARRELL

Slowly, in 2

JANITOR: Why are you cry - ing, daugh - ter?
MAGGIE: Friends, I've just seen a won - der

Why have you come? No need to be
with my own eyes. Our He - ro's tomb

a - fraid now, no need to run.
is emp - ty; I've been in - side.